Would You You Rather

Book For Kids

300+ Hilarious, Silly, and Challenging Questions To Make You Laugh

Stephen J. Ellis

Table Of Contents

Would You Rather?

Have you ever wondered what you'd do if you had to choose between something gross and something grosser? Or how you'd decide which superpower you'd rather have? How would you choose between never being able to cool down and never being able to warm up?

The **Would You Rather** game is meant to challenge you, make you laugh, and help you get to know your friends and family better. It's perfect for sleepovers, family game nights, and family vacations. You can even play it by yourself! Here's how it works:

Choose a category, then pick your favorite question and read it aloud. You can direct the question to a specific person or to the group as a whole. After they answer, pass the book to the person on your left and keep the game going. Everyone has to choose between the options they're given—that's what makes the game so fun!

Animals & Bugs

Animals can be cute, furry, and cuddly, but they can also be stinky or slimy. So which would you rather be? If you could, would you choose to have a dog the size of an elephant or an elephant the size of a dog? This section is about creatures of all kinds, so get ready to make some difficult choices!

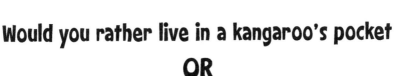
Would you rather live in a kangaroo's pocket

OR

have a pocket on your belly to keep a tiny kangaroo in?

Would you rather have a bamboo-only diet like a panda

OR

eat whatever you want but be covered in panda fur?

Would you rather slither on your belly like a snake

OR

walk on two legs but be covered in scales?

Would you rather find a
cockroach in your soup

OR

a spider in your shoe?

Would you rather croak like a frog but
eat whatever you want

OR

have your own voice but only eat bugs?

Would you rather laugh like a chipmunk

OR

belch every time you think something
is funny?

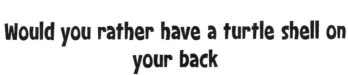
Would you rather have a turtle shell on your back

OR

a cat's tail?

Would you rather have a human body with a fishtail

OR

a fish body with human legs?

Would you rather get sprayed by a skunk once

OR

smell like B.O. every day for a month?

Would you rather be able to change your color like a chameleon

OR

breathe underwater like a fish?

Would you rather have sharp porcupine quills on your back

OR

have a shell-like an armadillo?

Would you rather be as big as a blue whale

OR

as small as a frog?

Would you rather have teeth like a crocodile

OR

have NO teeth, like an anteater?

Would you rather be as big as an elephant for one month

OR

be normal-sized but have elephant ears for one day?

Would you rather have a long neck like a giraffe

OR

sharp horns like a deer?

Would you rather be slow as a sloth

OR

be as fast as a cheetah?

Would you rather live in the cold
like a penguin

OR

live in the desert like a camel?

Would you rather hear as well as a bat

OR

see as well as an eagle?

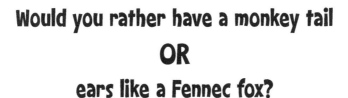
Would you rather have a monkey tail

OR

ears like a Fennec fox?

Would you rather be able to run
as fast as an ostrich

OR

climb trees like a koala?

Would you rather be a hamster for a day

OR

a rabbit?

Would you rather potty train a kitten
OR
teach a dog to use the toilet?

Would you rather sleep standing up
like a horse
OR
sleep with one eye open like a dolphin?

Would you rather eat poop like a dung beetle
OR
eat your own vomit like a housefly?

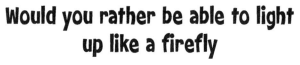
Would you rather be able to light
up like a firefly

OR

be able to spray your enemies with a smelly
fluid like a stink bug?

Would you rather be able to jump
as high as a grasshopper

OR

fly as fast as a dragonfly?

Would you rather have long legs
like a flamingo

OR

a long nose like an elephant?

Would you rather have webbed feet like a duck

OR

talons like a chicken?

Would you rather have spots on your skin like a ladybug

OR

have stripes like a zebra?

Would you rather be friends with a wolf

OR

have a lion as your worst enemy?

Would you rather collect honey with a bear
OR
go fishing with a seagull?

Would you rather have horns like a rhino
OR
a hard beak like a woodpecker?

Would you rather find a scorpion
in your bathtub
OR
an ant colony?

Would you rather be a parrot that can only say one word

OR

a gorilla that knows sign language?

Would you rather have a goose that laid golden eggs

OR

a duck that had diamond feathers?

Would you rather clean up elephant poo

OR

T-Rex vomit?

Would you rather milk a cow
OR
give a llama a haircut?

Food

What's the grossest food you've ever eaten? Would you be willing to eat it again if it meant you could have something you really wanted? Prepare for some really tough questions about some of your favorite—and least favorite—foods!

Would you rather only eat tuna for a month
OR
give up candy for six months?

Would you rather be allergic to chocolate
OR
allergic to tacos?

Would you rather eat salty candy
OR
sweet french fries?

Would you rather dip your french fries into chocolate ice cream

OR

dip your chicken nuggets into chocolate milk?

Would you rather eat 500 cookies in one day

OR

an entire apple pie in five minutes?

Would you rather have a refrigerator that always has your favorite foods inside

OR

an oven that automatically made your favorite meal once a week?

Would you rather eat a peanut butter
and egg sandwich

OR

eat jelly with your scrambled eggs?

Would you rather eat a booger once

OR

eat caviar on your pizza for a year?

Would you rather eat ice cream that
tastes like grass

OR

chew gum that tastes like a cheeseburger?

Would you rather eat macaroni with jelly beans

OR

cheese with oatmeal?

Would you rather eat a raw onion every day

OR

always have bad breath no matter what you eat?

Would you rather eat a grass-flavored hamburger

OR

a hot dog drizzled with caramel sauce?

Would you rather eat a hot dog drizzled
with chocolate syrup

OR

a donut covered in mustard?

Would you rather eat only really spicy food
every day for a month

OR

eat food with no flavor every day
for a year?

Would you rather drink spoiled milk

OR

eat cottage cheese with every meal?

Would you rather eat dinner for breakfast

OR

breakfast for dinner?

Would you rather have the sky rain ice cream

OR

have the ocean be made of your
favorite drink?

Would you rather eat tacos for every meal

OR

never be able to eat tacos again?

Would you rather eat chili with crickets instead of beans

OR

eat one chocolate-covered cricket?

Would you rather eat everything covered in cheese

OR

never eat cheese again?

Would you rather eat your least favorite cookie every day

OR

never eat your favorite cookie again?

Would you rather live the rest of your life without pizza

OR

without tacos?

Would you rather eat something that had mold on it

OR

eat something that had been soaked in vinegar?

Would you rather eat marshmallow pizza

OR

spaghetti tacos?

Would you rather eat everything
with chopsticks

OR

Only be able to use your fingers?

Would you rather eat alligator nuggets

OR

frog-leg soup?

Would you rather have to cook all your
food outside

OR

only be able to eat raw food?

Would you rather live in a house
made of candy

OR

a house made of fruit?

Would you rather only drink water and milk

OR

only drink soda that tastes like cucumbers?

Would you rather only eat fried
food forever

OR

only eat raw food?

Would you rather eat sushi every day for three months

OR

eat a raw snail one time?

Would you rather eat a lasagna cooked in the dishwasher

OR

a cookie baked on a hot blacktop?

Would you rather drink pickle juice once

OR

eat pickles with every meal for one month?

Would you rather eat a spoonful
of cinnamon

OR

a spoonful of pepper?

Would you rather eat at your favorite
fast-food restaurant every day

OR

eat dinner at a celebrity's house once?

Would you rather drink lemon juice
with breakfast

OR

lime juice with dinner?

Would You Rather For Kids

Would you rather eat fifty eggs in one day
OR
eat eggs with every meal for a year?

Would you rather eat soup from
the kitchen sink
OR
eat spaghetti with water instead of sauce?

Would you rather eat a cheeseburger
with a spider in it
OR
a slice of pizza with bug guts on top?

Would you rather eat dog food once
a day for a week

OR

eat cat food at every meal, every day
for a month?

Would you rather eat a chocolate cake
that fell in the dirt

OR

a slice of pie that's been in a dumpster?

Would you rather have a birthday cake
made of meatloaf

OR

a birthday cake made of fish sticks?

Would you rather only be able to eat orange foods

OR

only be able to eat green foods?

Would you rather eat ravioli filled with fish

OR

eat a donut filled with mayonnaise?

Would you rather eat pickle pancakes for every meal

OR

eat waffles filled with bubble gum?

Silly, Funny, & Weird

Ever wondered what it would be like to live in an alternate universe where humans smell with their ears and hear with their noses? If so, this section is for you! Buckle in because you might just learn a lot about your friends and family with these questions...

Would you rather have two mouths on your face

OR

one mouth on the back of your neck?

Would you rather meet a real leprechaun

OR

the tooth fairy?

Would you rather have a foot-long tongue

OR

feet the size of footballs?

Would you rather sleep hanging upside down
OR
sleep in a hammock made of spider silk?

Would you rather have hair that grows
an inch every day
OR
no eyelashes?

Would you rather get three wishes from a
genie but have to use them on someone else
OR
get one wish that you can use for yourself?

Would you rather have 20 sisters
OR
have 10 brothers?

Would you rather have blue eyebrows
OR
green ears?

Would you rather swim in a pool full of
chocolate pudding
OR
a pool full of ketchup?

Would you rather see a real dinosaur

OR

a real unicorn?

Would you rather find the end of a rainbow
and fight a leprechaun for his pot of gold

OR

find Bigfoot and become best friends?

Would you rather have to skip instead of walk

OR

have to sing instead of speak?

Would you rather have a car shaped like a hot dog

OR

a bicycle shaped like a pickle?

Would you rather have feet for hands

OR

hands for feet?

Would you rather know how to speak every language

OR

only speak one language but be able to communicate with aliens?

Would you rather only be able to use the bathroom once a day for a year

OR

go every ten minutes for a month?

Would you rather have the ability to fly for one day

OR

the ability to teleport for one hour?

Would you rather have eleven toes

OR

super long fingers?

Would you rather be invisible for a day

OR

have the ability to hear thoughts?

Would you rather have to ride a donkey to school every day

OR

ride in a clown car every day for a month?

Would you rather give up video games for a month

OR

only play the same game forever?

Would you rather lose your sense of smell
OR
lose your sense of taste?

Would you rather have a giant treehouse
made of candy
OR
a huge, in-ground swimming pool filled
with spaghetti?

Would you rather wash the dishes every night
OR
only eat with your hands for the rest
of your life?

Would you rather be itchy all the time
OR
have one itch you can never scratch?

Would you rather wake up early every day
OR
sleep in the bathtub every night for a year?

Would you rather always wear clothes you like
that are too big
OR
wear an ugly outfit to school every day
for a week?

Would you rather have a mustache made of spaghetti

OR

a beard you can never shave off?

Would you rather be super tall

OR

shrink down to the size of a bug?

Would you rather have teeth made of chocolate

OR

ears made of cheese?

Would you rather be able to bend your elbows but not your knees

OR

bend your knees but not your elbows?

Would you rather go over a tall bridge made of pretzels every day

OR

go through a tunnel carved from ice once a week?

The Hard Part

There are challenging questions, and then there are questions that really make you stop and think. This might take a while...

Would you rather be able to control the weather

OR

be able to invent your own holiday?

Would you rather have the ability to make people believe you no matter what you say

OR

be able to tell when someone is lying?

Would you rather wear a diaper for one week

OR

eat baby food for one day?

Would you rather have x-ray vision

OR

the ability to control fire and water?

Would you rather share a bedroom with someone for one year

OR

share a bathroom with someone for one week?

Would you rather be a racecar driver in a video game

OR

a horse jockey in real life?

Would you rather always speak in rhyme
OR
only hear other people speaking in rhyme?

Would you rather be able to meet your parents when they were kids
OR
meet your future self?

Would you rather have a water balloon fight without a towel
OR
a paintball fight with permanent paint?

Would you rather always be a little
late and be rich

OR

always be on time for things and be broke?

Would you rather jump off the tallest
diving board

OR

go down the tallest water slide?

Would you rather be a famous inventor

OR

a famous artist?

Would you rather have more hours in a day
OR
more days on the weekend?

Would you rather be trapped in your favorite video game
OR
trapped in your favorite movie?

Would you rather spend the night in a mall
OR
spend the night in a museum?

Would you rather be able to read minds

OR

be able to move things with your mind?

Would you rather only get five hours of sleep
every day for the rest of your life

OR

have to sleep for 16 hours every day for
three months?

Would you rather be stuck inside watching
movies you don't like

OR

get to go outside, but never watch
a movie again?

Would you rather be grounded for a month

OR

only get to go to the places your parents choose for a year?

Would you rather have your brain put into a robot's body for one month

OR

be able to live in the body of your favorite celebrity for one day?

Would you rather be a famous athlete

OR

a famous movie star?

Would you rather give up the internet
for one week

OR

give up your pet for one week?

Would you rather be the smartest kid
at school

OR

the most popular?

Would you rather explore outer space

OR

explore the deepest part of the ocean?

Would you rather go to the dentist
once a month

OR

never have to go again, but you have to
brush your teeth five times a day
for one year?

Would you rather be trapped on a desert
island with a stranger

OR

with someone you really dislike?

Would you rather have to get really dressed
up for school every day for a year

OR

stand up in front of your class and give a
presentation every day for a week?

Would you rather be jump-scared every time you get mad

OR

get hurt every time you're sad?

Would you rather take a vacation camping in the woods

OR

skiing on a mountain?

Would you rather be trapped in an elevator for two hours

OR

stuck in traffic for five hours?

Would you rather always have lint in your belly button

OR

only wear shirts that show your belly button?

Would you rather be a powerful wizard

OR

a superhero with only one power?

Would you rather never be able to get warm

OR

never be able to cool off?

Would you rather be able to walk
on the ceiling
OR
see through walls?

Would you rather trade bodies with a
grownup for one day
OR
stay the same age you are now for the next
three years?

Would you rather never have to do
homework again
OR
get paid to do it every day?

Would you rather win the lottery and take a smaller amount in one lump sum

OR

keep the full amount but have it broken up into monthly payments?

Would you rather step on a building block every day for a month

OR

lose your ability to taste sweets?

Would you rather have a video game design a character based on you

OR

have a movie made that is based on your life?

Would you rather mop the floor of your school's gym every day for a month

OR

wash the dishes at home every day for a year?

Would you rather have the hiccups every day for a year

OR

sneeze uncontrollably every day for a week?

Would you rather spend an entire day (with unlimited money) at the arcade

OR

spend the night at an aquarium?

Would you rather stay up late every night but never play your favorite video game

OR

play the game whenever you want, but have to go to bed early every night?

Would you rather be great at any card or board game

OR

be great at school work?

Would you rather be a talented gymnast

OR

be a talented ice skater?

Would you rather live in a city where it rains all the time

OR

live in a city where it's always cold and snowy?

Would you rather discover a real dragon

OR

dig up a real dinosaur skeleton?

Gross Out

If you've made it this far into the
book, chances are you're not easily
grossed out.

Let's put it to the test with some
questions that are meant

to challenge your gag reflex!

Would you rather always have burps that taste like old pizza

OR

always have the scent of onions on your hands?

Would you rather be completely hairless and smell great

OR

be covered in hair and smell like a skunk?

Would you rather vomit in class

OR

have someone from your class vomit on you?

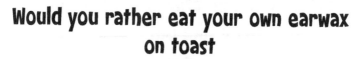

Would you rather eat your own earwax
on toast

OR

eat someone else's earwax in popsicle form?

Would you rather sweat ice cream

OR

cry tears made of honey?

Would you rather wash your hair with soap
scum every day for a month

OR

shave your head bald?

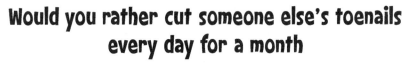

Would you rather cut someone else's toenails every day for a month

OR

not be able to cut your toenails for a year?

Would you rather drink a cup of someone else's sweat

OR

drink a gallon of your own?

Would you rather drink toilet water once

OR

lick the floor of a restaurant once a month?

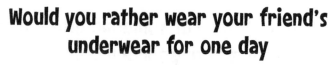

Would you rather wear your friend's underwear for one day

OR

wear the same pair of underwear for one month?

Would you rather use someone else's toothbrush

OR

someone else's used fork?

Would you rather take a bite of poo that tastes like cheese

OR

take a bite of cheese that tastes like poo?

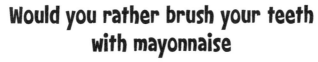

Would you rather brush your teeth
with mayonnaise

OR

floss with a celery string?

Would you rather have very loud farts that
don't smell

OR

silent farts that smell terrible?

Would you rather have a wedgie you can
never pull out

OR

never be able to blow your nose again?

Would you rather take a bath in mop water

OR

take a shower where the drain was clogged
with someone else's hair?

Creepy &
Spooky

Do you scare easily? Have a friend
who would rather lick a toad than be

in a room with a clown? Grab a
blanket to hide under and

settle in for some creepy questions...
if you dare.

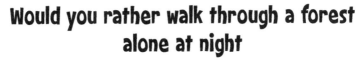

Would you rather walk through a forest alone at night

OR

spend one hour locked inside a coffin?

Would you rather spend three nights alone in a haunted castle

OR

spend one night in the castle with your least favorite person?

Would you rather be trapped in a house for two days with a clown

OR

trapped in a maze with a werewolf for one hour?

Would you rather watch a really scary
movie alone

OR

ride a scary roller coaster with a friend?

Would you rather be abducted by aliens

OR

have to live in a world with zombies?

Would you rather meet a ghost

OR

meet a sea monster?

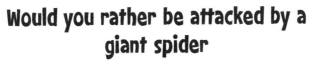

Would you rather be attacked by a
giant spider

OR

by a tiny skeleton?

Would you rather be attacked by
vampire bats

OR

stuck in a pit of snakes?

Would you rather be turned into a
frog by a witch

OR

turned into a bat by a vampire?

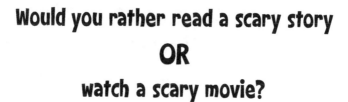
Would you rather read a scary story

OR

watch a scary movie?

Would you rather spend the night in an abandoned hospital

OR

walk through a graveyard at night alone?

Would you rather find a monster under your bed

OR

see a friendly ghost in your closet?

Would you rather have real vampire teeth
all the time

OR

turn into a werewolf once a month?

Would you rather sit in a tub filled with
cold pumpkin guts

OR

be dropped in a dunk tank filled with
slimy worms?

Would you rather kiss a toad

OR

keep a spider in your pocket?

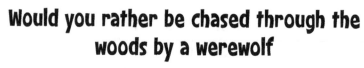

Would you rather be chased through the woods by a werewolf

OR

hide from zombies in a spooky old house?

Would you rather sleep in a room with a burping bat

OR

sleep in a room with a farting snake?

Would you rather walk through walls like a ghost

OR

be able to transform into an animal?

Would you rather be terrified of germs you can't see

OR

be scared of the dark?

Travel

Traveling can be exciting, but where would you go if you could choose any spot in the world? What if you could teleport to another planet or explore underwater caves with ease?

Use your imagination to answer these questions and more!

Would you rather be an astronaut
OR
a deep-sea diver?

Would you rather visit the jungle
OR
the desert?

Would you rather climb the tallest mountain
OR
explore the deepest cave?

Would you rather move to a new country where you didn't speak the language

OR

stay where you are and never be able to leave?

Would you rather fly in an airplane for six hours

OR

take a train ride for 12 hours?

Would you rather visit a tropical island

OR

an ancient city?

Would You Rather For Kids

Would you rather travel to Egypt and see the pyramids

OR

travel to Paris to see the Eiffel Tower?

Would you rather travel through time

OR

travel through outer space?

Would you rather drive around the country for three months

OR

travel around the world for one year?

Would you rather fly in a hot air balloon

OR

sail on a boat?

Would you rather go on a camping
trip for two weeks

OR

go to a luxury spa?

Would you rather visit the beach but never
go into the ocean

OR

stay home and swim in a pool once?

Would you rather take your dream vacation
with only $50 spending money

OR

visit a place you've never heard of
with unlimited money?

Would you rather swim with dolphins
in Hawaii

OR

climb to the top of the Statue Of Liberty?

Would you rather travel 100 years
into the future

OR

100 years into the past?

Would you rather walk on Mars

OR

sleep on Saturn?

Would you rather be able to fly

OR

have the ability to teleport?

Would you rather forget to pack clean
underwear for a trip

OR

forget to pack your favorite device?

Would you rather get lost in a foreign city

OR

never be able to travel outside your own city?

Would you rather take a trip with your favorite author

OR

with your favorite singer?

Would you rather visit Tokyo with your best friend

OR

visit Australia with your family?

Would You Rather For Kids

Would you rather find a magic door that led to an alternate universe

OR

find a magic car that would take you anywhere in the world?

Would you rather take a trip to the moon in a space shuttle

OR

take a trip to the bottom of the ocean in a submarine?

Would you rather be stuck on a bus with a weird smell for 12 hours

OR

be stuck on a plane with a crying baby for six hours?

Would you rather ride in a helicopter over the Grand Canyon

OR

take the subway in New York City?

Would you rather play with penguins in Antarctica

OR

ride on the back of an elephant in Africa?

Would you rather go searching for buried treasure

OR

dig up dinosaur bones?

Would you rather take a trip on a cruise ship for one week

OR

sail on a yacht for one month?

Would you rather go on a shopping spree in a candy shop for one hour in France

OR

go on a shopping spree in a toy store for five minutes in Australia?

Technology & Science

Have you ever wondered what it would be like to live in an era without video games?

How would you choose between being able to watch television and being able to get online? This section is for all you kids who can't go a day without tech!

Would you rather only be able to watch one television channel of your choosing

OR

only be able to get online?

Would you rather spend a week without a computer

OR

one day without your phone?

Would you rather live on a planet without gravity

OR

on a planet without a sun?

Would you rather live in a city with
man-eating plants

OR

in a city full of plants that smell
like rotting garbage?

Would you rather have a purple sky

OR

have clouds that look like dinosaurs?

Would you rather have a telescope that
shows you distant planets

OR

a microscope that shows you tiny worlds?

Would you rather be caught outside
in a rainstorm

OR

be stuck inside because of a snowstorm?

Would you rather be stuck in a crater on
the moon for one day

OR

be stuck in a crater on a volcano
for one hour?

Would you rather live in a world
without YouTube

OR

in a world without your favorite
game console?

Would you rather have the technology to create a flying car

OR

to create time travel?

Would you rather have a device to communicate with animals

OR

a device that allows you to communicate with famous people in history?

Would you rather have a "smart" house that does everything for you

OR

an old-fashioned mansion with a pool and game room?

Would You Rather For Kids

Would you rather only eat foods that can be cooked in a microwave

OR

only eat foods that can be cooked over an open fire?

Would you rather ride in a self-driving car

OR

have to teleport everywhere?

Would you rather invent a device that lets you see one day into your own future

OR

one YEAR into someone else's future?

Would you rather have all of today's technology but only be able to use it for an hour a day

OR

have to only use technology from the 1970's?

Would you rather study creatures from space

OR

creatures from the bottom of the sea?

Would you rather be an astronaut for a week

OR

a deep-sea diver for a month?

School

Whether you love it or hate it, school is just a part of life. What would you do if you ran things instead of the principal?

How would you choose between no homework and sleeping in?

Here are some questions that might make you wish you could turn them into a reality...

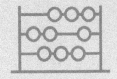

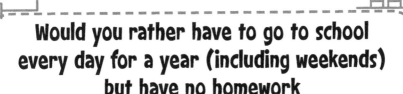

Would you rather have to go to school
every day for a year (including weekends)
but have no homework

OR

get weekends off but have homework every day?

Would you rather perform onstage
for a huge crowd

OR

show up at school in your pajamas?

Would you rather be principal for one day

OR

teach your favorite class?

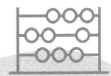

Would you rather never have homework again
OR
be able to sleep in an extra hour every day?

Would you rather be able to eat lunch outside
OR
choose what was on the menu?

Would you rather make straight A's
OR
be great at a school sport?

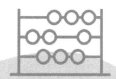

Would you rather play a prank on your favorite teacher

OR

play a prank on your friend and not get caught?

Would you rather have a two-hour recess every day

OR

have an extra day off during a holiday?

Would you rather make up the school rules

OR

add something fun to your school, like a swimming pool?

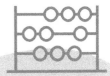

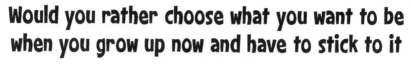

Would you rather choose what you want to be when you grow up now and have to stick to it

OR

have someone else choose your grownup job for you?

Would you rather throw a pie at your favorite teacher's face

OR

have someone throw a pie at your face in front of the whole school?

Would you rather go to gym class

OR

go to art class?

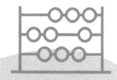

Would you rather ride the bus to school every day

OR

walk to school even if the weather is bad?

Would you rather be able to choose where you sit in class

OR

be able to choose your teacher next year?

Would you rather take a field trip to the zoo

OR

a field trip to the aquarium?

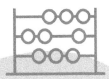

Would you rather pack the same
lunch every day
OR
eat in the cafeteria even when they cook
something you don't like?

Would you rather be the class clown
OR
the teacher's pet?

Would you rather be late to class every day
OR
be on time but never have a pencil?

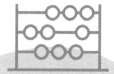

Would you rather wear a uniform to school
OR
wear clothes you wore last year?

Would you rather take a silly yearbook picture
OR
take a good picture, but your eyes
are closed?

Would you rather have to attend school
wearing a clown wig
OR
wearing clown shoes?

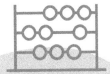

Would you rather have a mean
substitute teacher

OR

have a mean principal?

Would you rather watch a movie in
class once a week

OR

have a party in class every month?

Would you rather take a test every day

OR

never have to do homework again?

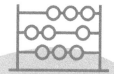

Would you rather only be able to use the swings at recess

OR

only be able to use the slide?

Would you rather have to wear your pajamas to school

OR

clothes from the lost and found?

Would you rather have a part in the school play

OR

play an instrument?

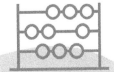

Would you rather be the last person picked to play flag football

OR

the first person hit in dodgeball?

Would you rather spill chocolate milk on yourself at lunch

OR

get mud on the back of your pants at recess?

Would you rather sing a solo in music class

OR

be called on to do math at the front of the class?

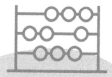

Would you rather burp loudly in the library
OR
fart silently in gym class?

Holidays & Seasons

What's your favorite holiday? Would you be able to choose between giving it up and having unlimited screen time?

Get ready to make some hard choices!

Would you rather go trick-or-treating in a costume you hate

OR

have to skip trick-or-treating next year?

Would you rather give up half your holiday gifts

OR

have to go to school all year with no breaks?

Would you rather live in a state where it never snowed

OR

in a state where it always rained?

Would you rather eat Halloween candy
OR
Christmas candy?

Would you rather wear holiday ornaments on your clothes to school
OR
sing holiday songs in front of your class?

Would you rather eat Christmas cookies for a month
OR
Thanksgiving food for a week?

Would you rather work in Santa's workshop
OR
help him deliver gifts?

Would you rather have a snowball fight
OR
build a gingerbread house?

Would you rather wrap 100 presents
OR
bake 100 cookies?

Would you rather grow a Santa beard you can't shave off

OR

grow elf ears you can never get rid of?

Would you rather stay home for the holidays and get lots of gifts

OR

go to your favorite theme park but get no gifts?

Would you rather drink hot chocolate with every meal in summer

OR

drink lemonade with every meal in winter?

Would you rather have a Christmas vacation

OR

summer vacation?

Would you rather eat so much at Thanksgiving that your clothes don't fit

OR

get so much candy at Halloween that you can't eat it all before it goes bad?

Would you rather listen to Christmas songs every day for two months

OR

sing Christmas songs every day for a month?

Would You Rather For Kids

Would you rather get one big present
OR
lots of little ones?

Would you rather watch holiday movies
OR
Halloween movies?

Would you rather know what all your gifts are ahead of time
OR
only receive gifts you didn't ask for?

Would you rather wear an ugly Christmas sweater to school

OR

wear your Halloween costume?

Would you rather spend the holidays skiing at a cabin in the mountains

OR

relaxing on a beach?

Would you rather go on vacation during spring break

OR

stay home and play video games all week?

Would you rather read 20 books over the summer

OR

read 2 books over Christmas break?

Would you rather jump in a pile of leaves

OR

make snow angels?

Would you rather swim in the ocean

OR

swim in a pool at a resort?

Would you rather spend the summer traveling in an RV with your family

OR

hanging out at home with your best friend?

Would you rather stay in a fancy hotel

OR

on a big, fancy boat?

Would you rather go snorkeling on spring break

OR

go to the water park on summer break?

Would you rather eat popsicles
in the winter

OR

chili in the summer?

Would you rather make friends with a polar
bear who tells hilarious jokes

OR

with a reindeer who can fly you anywhere?

Would you rather go all summer without
using a computer

OR

go all summer without using a pool?

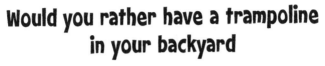
Would you rather have a trampoline
in your backyard

OR

an outdoor movie theater?

Would you rather give up air conditioning
for an entire summer

OR

keep the A/C but never be able to go
swimming again?

Would you rather have a stinky sock full of
money as a Christmas stocking

OR

a regular stocking filled with candy?

Would you rather never go
trick-or-treating again

OR

give up your holiday gifts once?

Would you rather ride in an airplane

OR

ride in Santa's sleigh?

Would you rather go ice skating on Christmas

OR

water skiing on summer break?

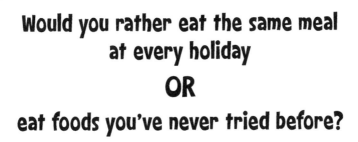

Would you rather eat the same meal
at every holiday
OR
eat foods you've never tried before?

Would you rather visit the pumpkin patch
OR
the Easter bunny?

Would you rather eat 20 Easter eggs
OR
give up your Easter basket for the year?

Would you rather watch a fireworks show
OR
have a sleepover with your friends?

Would you rather have an unlimited amount
of sparklers
OR
an unlimited amount of sidewalk chalk?

Next Read

Don't miss the second book of this series...

Would You Rather Game Book For Kids

250+ Silly, Hilarious, and Challenging Scenarios The Whole Family Will Love

Go To The Below URL:

www.thestephenellis.com/wur2

Want More Books By Stephen Ellis?

Go To The Below URL:

www.thestephenellis.com/books

notes